Classifying Birds

ANDREW SOLWAY

Heinemann
LIBRARY

www.heinemann.co.uk/library

Visit our website to find out more information about Heinemann Library books.

To order:
☎ Phone 44 (0) 1865 888066
📄 Send a fax to 44 (0) 1865 314091
💻 Visit the Heinemann Bookshop at www.heinemann.co.uk/library to browse our catalogue and order online.

First published in Great Britain by Heinemann Library, Halley Court, Jordan Hill, Oxford OX2 8EJ, part of Harcourt Education. Heinemann is a registered trademark of Harcourt Education Ltd.

Editorial: Jilly Attwood and Jennifer Tubbs
Design: Jo Hinton-Malivoire and AMR
Illustrations: Josephine Blake and David Woodroffe
Picture Research: Catherine Bevan, Hannah Taylor and Su Alexander
Production: Séverine Ribierre

Originated by Dot Gradations Ltd
Printed in Hong Kong, China by Wing King Tong

ISBN 0 431 16780 X
07 06 05 04 03
10 9 8 7 6 5 4 3 2 1

British Library Cataloguing in Publication Data
Solway, Andrew
Classifying Living Things – Birds
598'.012
A full catalogue record for this book is available from the British Library.

Acknowledgements
For Harriet, Eliza and Nicholas.

The publishers would like to thank the following for permission to reproduce photographs: Corbis: 22 (Eric and David Hosking), 24 (Fritz Polking), 27 (Francis G. Mayer); Digital Stock: 20; Digital Vision: 4 (right), 17; Natural History Museum: 29 (Michael Long); Nature Picture Library: 11 (John Downer), 16 (John Cancalosi), 21 (John Cancalosi); Oxford Scientific Film: 4 (left) (Robert Tyrell), 7 (David M. Dennis), 9 (Michael Dick/AA), 12 (Mark Hamblin), 13 (Norbert Rosing), 14 (Daniel Cox), 15 (Mary Plage), 18 (Kjell Sandved), 19 (Doug Allen), 23 (Robert Tyrell), 25 (Daybreak Imagery), 26 (Konrad Wothe); Photodisc: 5.

Cover photograph of white pelicans reproduced with permission of Oxford Scientific Films.

The publishers would like to thank Martin Lawrence, museum educator, for his assistance in the preparation of this book.

Every effort has been made to contact copyright holders of any material reproduced in this book. Any omissions will be rectified in subsequent printings if notice is given to the publishers.

Contents

Words in the text in bold, **like this**, are explained in the Glossary.

The variety of life

The world is full of an incredible variety of living things. They range from tiny bacteria, too small to see, to huge redwood trees, over 100 metres tall. With such a bewildering variety of life, it's hard to make sense of the living world. So scientists classify living things – they sort them into groups.

Sorting the living world

When you sort something, you need to do it in the right way. Scientists try to classify living things in a way that shows how one group of animals or plants is related to another.

Scientists who sort birds look at all kinds of differences between them, from the colour of their feathers to the shape of their bones. They also look at **fossils** of birds that lived in the past, to see which modern birds they are like. From all this information, they decide which birds are closely related, and which are not.

From kingdoms to species

Classification works like this. First, scientists divide living things up into huge groups called **kingdoms**. Plants, for example, are all in one kingdom, while all animals are in another.

Birds range in size from tiny hummingbirds to ostriches, which can grow up to a huge 2.5 metres tall.

Each kingdom is divided into smaller groups called **phyla** (singular phylum), and phyla are further divided into **classes**. The next subdivision is into **orders**, then come **families**, then **genera** (singular genus), and finally **species**. A species is a single kind of animal or plant, such as a swallow or a buttercup.

Scientific names

Many living things have a common name. But common names are not always exact. The bird called a robin in Europe, for instance, is different from an American robin.

To sort out these problems, scientists give every species of living thing a two-part name. The two names are a bit like your first name and surname. The first name is the name of the genus that the creature belongs to. The second is the name of the species within that genus.

Using scientific names, it's easy to tell the two types of robin apart. The American robin has the name *Turdus migratorius*, while the European robin is *Erithacus rubecula*.

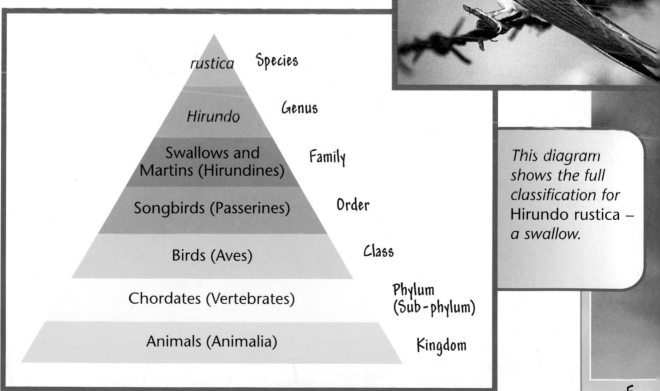

rustica	Species
Hirundo	Genus
Swallows and Martins (Hirundines)	Family
Songbirds (Passerines)	Order
Birds (Aves)	Class
Chordates (Vertebrates)	Phylum (Sub-phylum)
Animals (Animalia)	Kingdom

This diagram shows the full classification for Hirundo rustica – a swallow.

What are birds?

We classify living things according to how closely they are related. Birds are all related to each other because they all have one group of **ancestors** that lived millions of years ago.

How birds fit in

Birds are part of the animal **kingdom**. Animals, unlike plants, cannot make their own food and must eat other living things to stay alive. Birds are part of a group called the **vertebrates**. Like us, birds have backbones. This is what makes them vertebrates.

Evolving and adapting

Over thousands or millions of years, groups of living things change, or evolve, to fit in better with their environment (the place they live). This happens because living things that are better **adapted** (suited) to their environment, live longer and produce more offspring. All the birds we see today have evolved from a single ancestor.

What makes a bird a bird?

Scientists have found several key differences between birds and other vertebrates. By looking at all the differences together, we can tell whether an animal is a bird or not.

Other vertebrates may have smooth skin, or they may be scaly or hairy. But birds are the only animals that have feathers. Most vertebrates have bony jaws, and usually teeth as well. Birds, however, all have a horny beak.

Fossils teach us about birds that lived millions of years ago. This bird, Archaeopteryx, lived about 150 million years ago. It had wings and feathers, but its beak had teeth and it had claws on its legs.

All birds have wings. Even birds that can't fly, such as ostriches, have small wings. Bats also have wings, but their wings are not covered with feathers.

Birds are divided into about 27 different **orders**. This table shows the main bird orders and those mentioned in this book.

Order	No. of species	Examples
Anseriformes	150	ducks, geese and swans
Apodiformes	403	swifts and hummingbirds
Charadriiformes	257	gulls, terns, skuas, auks, snipes, sandpipers, plovers and other shore birds
Ciconiiformes	1,033	storks, herons, flamingos
Columbiformes	316	pigeons, doves and sandgrouse
Coraciiformes	193	kingfishers, bee-eaters, rollers and hornbills
Cuculiformes	151	cuckoos
Falconiformes	286	eagles, falcons, hawks, vultures, osprey and secretary bird
Galliformes	256	grouse, pheasants, partridges, quails, turkeys and junglefowl
Gruiformes	197	cranes, rails and bustards
Passeriformes	5,200	sparrows, starlings, robins, finches, warblers, tits, ovenbirds, tyrant flycatchers, swallows and martins, wagtails, shrikes, thrushes
Piciformes	376	woodpeckers, jacamars, puffbirds, barbets, honeyguides and toucans
Psittaciformes	130	parrots, cockatoos, budgerigars, lovebirds and macaws
Strigiformes	134	owls
Struthioniformes	14	ostriches, emus

Feathers

Birds are the only living things that have feathers. A bird would not be a bird without them. Feathers grow from a bird's skin in the same way that we grow hair or nails.

A bird's feathers do three important jobs:
- they give the bird a smooth, streamlined shape. This makes flying through the air easy, saving the bird's energy
- feathers on the bird's skinny 'arms' turn them into broad, flexible wings, ideal for flying
- feathers on its body protect the skin from the sun in hot weather and keep it warm in cold weather.

Feather structure

Feathers have a structure that makes them very light and strong. Down the centre of the feather is a hollow tube or rib. Sticking out from this rib are hundreds of thin, slanting strips called barbs. Each barb has rows of tiny teeth along its length, which link up with the teeth of the barbs on either side like the teeth in a zip. This locks the barbs together, to make the feather into a strong, flat blade.

In wing feathers, all the barbs link together in this way. But on the body, the lower part of each feather is soft and fluffy. The fluffy (downy) part of the feather helps keep the bird warm.

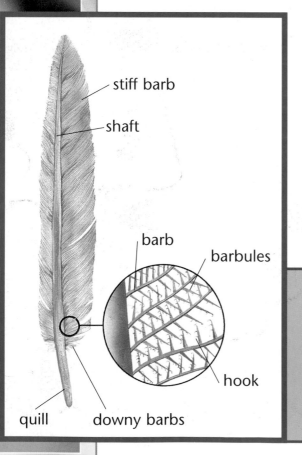

stiff barb

shaft

barb

barbules

hook

quill   downy barbs

The parts of a feather (this is a body feather). The enlargement shows how the teeth on each barb lock together. Each barb has lots of even tinier teeth, called barbules, on it. The barbules have 'hooks' on them that zip up the barbules.

Feathers are tough, but they must be looked after and they do wear out. Birds regularly preen (clean and comb their feathers with their beak). Then about once a year, birds moult (their old feathers are replaced with new ones).

Patterns and colours

A bird's plumage (its feathers) can be almost any colour, from dull browns and greys to bright reds and blues. The plumage may help the bird **camouflage** itself. Birds that live in reeds, for instance, often have a pattern of brown and black bars that makes them very hard to spot among the reeds.

But some birds have plumage that really stands out. They are usually male birds, and they grow brightly coloured feathers to help them attract females for **breeding**. In some birds, the breeding feathers can be truly spectacular.

Birds of paradise, like this Wilson's bird of paradise, live in warm tropical forests in Australia and New Guinea. The males have spectacular feathers, which they parade in the breeding season to attract females.

Built to fly

We have already seen that a bird's wing feathers help it to fly. But there is much more to flying than wings and feathers. From beak to tail, inside and out, birds are suited for flight.

Light bones

Compared to a land animal of the same size, a bird's skeleton is lighter and stronger. This helps it to fly. One way that a bird's skeleton is different is that it has fewer bones. Many of the bones in its back and pelvis (hips) are fused (joined together). A bird's wings also have fewer bones than the arms or front feet of other **vertebrates**.

A bird's beak is another **adaptation** to save weight. Jawbones and teeth are much heavier than a bird's light, strong beak. Birds have also lost their tail bones, which has helped to balance their skeleton.

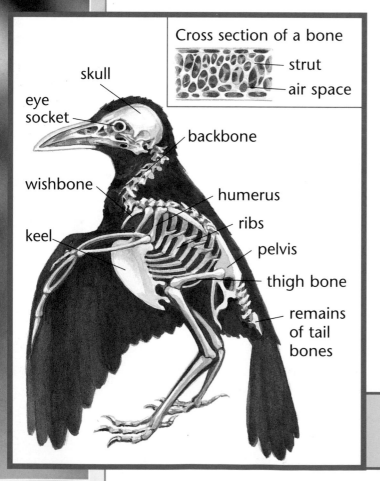

Cross section of a bone

- strut
- air space

skull
eye socket
backbone
wishbone
humerus
ribs
keel
pelvis
thigh bone
remains of tail bones

In many birds, the bones themselves are lighter than those of other animals. This is because they have air spaces inside them. Bigger birds usually have more air spaces in their bones than smaller ones. A frigate bird, for example, has a wingspan of over 2 metres, but its skeleton weighs less than its feathers! Even birds that have lost the ability to fly have fewer bones in their skeleton and a beak instead of jaws.

The skeleton of a bird.

Strong muscles

Although birds are light, they still need a lot of muscle power to get into the air. Nearly all a bird's muscles are concentrated in its body, because heavy

*Every year, bar-headed geese fly over Mount Everest, at heights of over 9000 metres, on their **migration** flights. At this height there is only a third of the amount of oxygen in the air that there is at sea level.*

muscles in the wings would make them harder to flap. The biggest muscles are the breast muscles, which flap the wings. They are attached to a broad, flat bone fastened to the ribs, called the keel.

A bird's legs also need strong muscles to absorb the shock of landing. All these muscles are concentrated at the tops of the legs – the legs themselves are very skinny. Flightless birds have leg muscles that are big and strong, but the muscles in the upper body are much reduced as they don't need them for flying.

Energy for flying

Birds need a strong heart and a good blood system to keep their muscles supplied with energy. Hummingbird hearts beat fastest of all: up to 1200 times every minute! Human hearts beat about 70 times per minute. On a high mountain, humans find it hard to breathe, because there is less oxygen high in the atmosphere, but birds have no problems flying at these heights. They have very efficient lungs, which can get more oxygen from the air.

Perching birds

Over half the bird **species** in the world are perching birds or **passerines**. They all have feet suited for perching, with three toes pointing forwards and a strong fourth toe pointing backwards. Most passerines are small or medium-sized. One or two species feed in water, but most are land birds.

Although passerines have some things in common, they come in a fantastic variety of colours, shapes and sizes. Many common birds – for example crows, finches, sparrows, swallows, tits, thrushes and wrens – are passerines. But the group also includes the fabulously decorated birds of paradise, **nectar**-eating sunbirds and impressive nest-builders such as ovenbirds and weaver birds.

Songbirds

One large group of passerines are the songbirds. All birds have short calls to keep in touch or to warn of danger. In some species, male birds have songs that they sing to mark out their territory or to attract a **mate**. But only songbirds have extra muscles in their voice box to help them sing. Not all songbirds are good singers. Few people would call the harsh croak of a crow beautiful, but crows are songbirds!

Larks are quite dull-looking brown birds, but when the male lark opens its beak and starts to sing, its song is beautiful.

Passerine foods

Most passerines eat seeds or insects – or both. For instance, sparrows and finches mostly eat seeds, swallows and martins catch insects in flight, and crows and their relatives eat both kinds of food. A few passerines eat other foods, though. Sunbirds are like hummingbirds and eat nectar from flowers. Birds of paradise eat fruit. In the tropical forests where they live, there are trees in fruit all year.

Nest-builders

Many passerines lay their eggs in cup-like nests or domed nests that are completely enclosed. The young are blind and helpless when they hatch. Some passerines are impressive nest-builders. Male weaver birds thread together grass and plant stems to make basket-like nests. Ovenbirds build domed clay nests, which look similar to the clay ovens that people sometimes make to cook food outdoors.

A golden pale weaver building a nest in Mombasa, Kenya. Male weavers build nests to attract females. A female will mate with the male whose nest she likes best.

Food grinder

Birds have no teeth, so they cannot chew their food. Without chewing, it is very difficult for the **digestive system** to get nutrients (nourishment) from food. So birds 'chew' their food in their stomachs! A part of the stomach called the gizzard has very hard, muscular walls. In the gizzard, the food is churned around and ground up into small pieces. To help the gizzard do its work, most birds swallow small stones or grit.

Living on the ground

Quite a few birds have lost the ability to fly, but ostriches and their relatives are a whole group of birds that are flightless. Game birds are another **order** of ground-dwellers. They are similar in some ways to ostriches and their relatives, although many of them can fly. Pheasants, quails, partridges, grouse and Indian junglefowl (chicken **ancestors**) are all game birds.

Cassowaries are nearly as big as ostriches. They have a deadly kick, and the inner nail on their feet can be 10 centimetres long. More people in New Guinea are killed by cassowaries than by any other wild animal.

Ostriches

Ostriches, cassowaries, emus and rheas are all large birds with long, powerful legs. Ostriches, emus and rheas live in open country and are fast runners, while cassowaries are forest birds. They all feed mainly on plants and nest on the ground.

Kiwis are much smaller than their ostrich relatives, and move more slowly. They hunt at night for earthworms, their favourite food. Although their eyesight is poor, they have an excellent sense of smell.

Birds like elephants!

Ostriches are the biggest living birds. They can grow up to 2.5 metres tall and weigh twice as much as an average man. Until a few hundred years ago in New Zealand there were much bigger birds called moas. The biggest grew to almost 4 metres in height. That's taller than an elephant!

Game birds

Birds such as pheasants, grouse, partridges and quails have for many years been bred and hunted for sport. This is why they are called 'game' birds. The scientific name for them is the Galliformes. Game birds live on open ground or in forests, hunting for seeds and other plant food. They usually hide if danger threatens, but if they spot a predator (hunting animal) they suddenly burst out and fly quickly upwards. A grouse can fly almost vertically from the ground.

Female game birds are usually dull-coloured, but some males have splendid coats of feathers (plumage). The peahen for example has plain, brown plumage whereas the peacock is famous for its dazzling display of colourful feathers.

Like ostriches, most game birds nest on the ground. If their young were born helpless like those of **passerines**, they would soon be snapped up by predators. To avoid this, the young have feathers when they hatch and are ready to move about and feed themselves. They can fly within a day of hatching.

In the **breeding** season, male sage grouse gather on open ground at dawn. They puff themselves up, leap, flutter and pose to try and attract females. This behaviour is known as lekking.

Storks,

Storks, h
long-legg
The grou
ibises. He
spear usir
a kind of
them to s
Flamingo:
creatures
to make l
they nest

Pelicans

Pelicans, g
well as wa
toes, and
net, scoop
out. Corm
down in h
pouch that

Birds in thi
tactics. The
make them

Seabirds and shore birds

Most seabirds belong to one of three bird **orders**: gulls and waders, tube-nosed birds and penguins.

Gulls and waders

This order of birds includes seabirds such as gulls and terns, shorebirds such as sandpipers and plovers, and swimming birds such as puffins and auks. They do not look similar, but they are grouped together because they have similar skulls, backbones and voice boxes.

Terns and auks eat fish, but gulls are often scavengers, feeding on almost anything left by others. Waders feed on shores and in shallow water, digging in soft mud for worms and other creatures. Gulls and waders nest on the ground, often in a small hollow scraped by the bird.

Tube-nosed birds

Tube-nosed birds include albatrosses, petrels and shearwaters. Most animals cannot drink seawater because of the salt in it. Seabirds have glands in their nose that can remove the salt, and these glands are particularly big in tube-nosed birds. Many tube-nosed birds spend almost their whole lives feeding on the open ocean, coming to land only to **breed**.

Skimmers are close relatives of gulls. They feed by skimming low, with the bottom part of their beak in the water. If they feel a fish, they snap it up.

Swans are st... fliers, but ha... trouble takin... They have to... the water to... speed for tak...

Penguins

More than any other birds, penguins have made the sea their home. They cannot fly, and their wings have become short flippers that they use for swimming. Penguins live mostly in cold seas in the southern hemisphere (half of the world). As protection against the cold they have short, fur-like feathers and a thick layer of fat, or blubber.

Penguins come to shore mainly to breed. They usually breed in **colonies**, laying one or two eggs on a heap of stones or in a burrow. Emperor and king penguins make no nest at all. Male emperor penguins put the single egg on their feet, and cover it with a special flap of skin to keep it warm.

Marathon migration

Many birds **migrate** each year. They breed in cooler climates, then migrate in autumn to warmer places, where there is more food during the winter. Many birds migrate long distances, but Arctic terns fly furthest of all. They spend half the year in the Arctic, then fly right across the world to the Antarctic, a one-way trip of over 16,000 kilometres.

Emperor penguins breed in the Antarctic. The female penguin lays a single egg, then returns to the sea, leaving the male to look after it. When the egg hatches two months later, the female returns to help feed the chick.

Birds of prey

Birds of **prey** are birds that catch animals or other birds for food. They have strong talons (claws) for gripping their prey and hooked beaks that are good for tearing flesh. There are two orders: the hawks and falcons, which mostly hunt by day, and the owls, which usually hunt by night.

Hawks and falcons

Eagles, buzzards, hawks, falcons and Old World vultures all belong to this group of birds. Old World vultures do not usually catch their own prey – they eat carrion (dead animals). All hawks and falcons have excellent eyesight, and some vultures also have a good sense of smell.

Most hawks and falcons swoop down on their prey and grab them in their strong talons, then kill them with their sharp beaks. Some birds hunt from a perch, others glide and soar over an area, looking for prey. Falcons dive from a height on to flying birds. They reach speeds of up to 130 kilometres an hour. The prey is hit so hard that the impact kills it.

Ospreys hunt fish. They plunge talons-first into the water when they see a likely meal. Fish are slippery creatures, so ospreys have studs on their toes for extra grip.

Owls can lay up to twelve eggs. The eggs do not all hatch at once. If there is not enough food to feed all the young, the smallest ones do not get as much food. Eventually they die and are eaten by the others.

Owls

Like hawks and falcons, owls have hooked beaks and strong talons. But they look very different, with two large eyes in a round or heart-shaped face.

An owl's eyes are designed to see well in very dim light. But even more important for night hunting are its ears. These are hidden under the feathers just below its eyes. The shape of the owl's face is designed to collect sounds and focus them on the ears. The ears can also tell where a sound is coming from. In territory it knows, an owl can hunt in the dark using its hearing alone.

An owl's wing-feathers have soft fringes at the tips, which soften the sound the owl makes as it flaps its wings. This means that the owl's victims do not hear it coming. It also allows the owl to hear the movements of prey animals.

Owls usually eat their prey whole. They cannot digest the animal's bones or fur, so after they have digested a meal, they cough up a small pellet of this undigested matter. Scientists often look at these pellets to find out what an owl has been eating.

Flying aces

Although many birds are brilliant fliers, none are more impressive than the swifts and hummingbirds. Swifts spend almost their whole life in flight, catching insects in their wide-open mouths as they flit through the air. Hummingbirds are far better than other birds at hovering in one place, and they can fly backwards. Nightjars are aerial acrobats like swifts, but as their name suggests they hunt at night.

Swifts and hummingbirds

Swifts and hummingbirds are related by their short legs and tiny feet. Some swifts have such small legs and feet that they cannot walk on flat ground.

Swifts are smallish birds with long, pointed wings. They catch insects, sleep and even **mate** in the air. The only time they land is when they are nesting. Swifts' nests are usually high up, sometimes in the roof of a building. The nest is made from small twigs and other material, held together with saliva (spit).

The nests of cave swiftlets in South-east Asia are made completely of saliva. In China, people make cave swiftlet nests into bird's nest soup.

Hummingbirds are colourful birds with long bills. Their main food is **nectar**, which they suck from flowers with their tube-like tongues. They also eat insects. They build tiny, neat cup nests which they stick together using spiders' webs.

Some hummingbirds live in tropical areas, where there are flowers all year, but others migrate. A hummingbird's wings beat very fast: up to 80 times in a second. When it hovers, the hummingbird rotates its wings as they beat, moving them in a figure-of-eight pattern. This is why it can hover so well.

Nightjars

Like swifts, most nightjars catch insects whilst in flight. They hunt mostly at night and moths are the main food for many **species**. Nightjars have small beaks but they can open their mouths very wide. Some species are known as frogmouths because of this. During the day, nightjars rest on the ground or in trees, relying on their excellent **camouflage** to keep them safe from enemies.

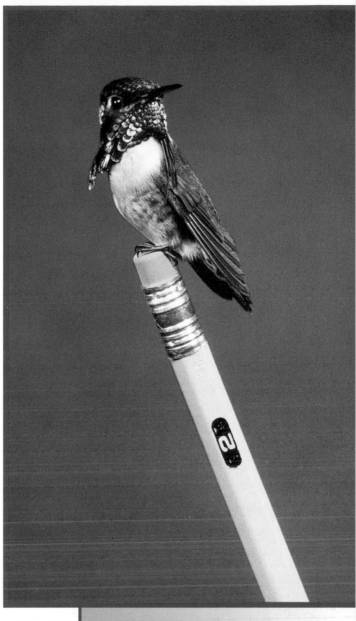

All hummingbirds are small, but some are really tiny. The bee hummingbird is less than 6 centimetres from beak to tail and its body is not much bigger than that of a bee.

Hole-nesters

Woodpeckers and kingfishers belong to two **orders** of birds that lay their eggs in holes. Many kingfishers dig their holes in earth banks or rotten trees. Woodpeckers use their strong bills to hack out nesting holes in tree trunks.

Kingfishers and relatives

Kingfishers and their relatives are often brightly coloured. The order includes bee-eaters, rollers and hornbills. Most of them perch and watch for food, then swoop or dive to catch it.

Rollers swoop on insects or small creatures and sometimes also eat fruit. Kingfishers are mostly water birds, diving from a perch to stab fish with their beaks. Bee-eaters catch flying insects, especially bees and wasps.

Kingfishers and their relatives lay between two and seven eggs. Their young are born blind and helpless. Female hornbills use mud to block up the entrance to their nest hole, leaving only a narrow opening. The mother then lays her eggs and incubates them (keeps them warm). The male feeds her through the small nest opening. After the eggs hatch, the mother stays sealed in with the nestlings (young) until they are no longer helpless. Then at last she breaks the nest open.

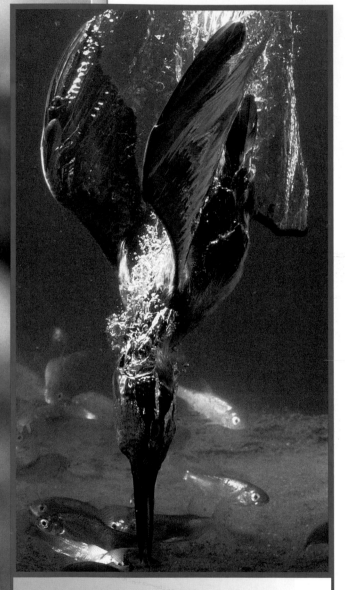

A common kingfisher plunge-dives for food. Although kingfishers are common in many parts of the world, the white-collared kingfisher of Arabia is one of the rarest birds on Earth. Only about 50 pairs are known to survive.

Woodpeckers

Woodpeckers and their relatives include jacamars, puffbirds, barbets, honeyguides and toucans. They are often brightly coloured or have strong markings. All of them have feet with two backward-pointing toes and two toes pointing forwards. They nest in holes and lay pure white eggs.

Woodpeckers feed at tree trunks, poking their beaks into cracks in the bark and licking out insects with their super-long tongues. Woodpeckers' stiff tails help them to balance on tree trunks as they move around. Jacamars and puffbirds chase after flying insects, such as bee-eaters, while barbets eat fruit and insects.

Honeyguides like to eat the wax from bees' nests. But they can't open bees' nests themselves, so they get help. If a honeyguide finds a bees' nest, it flies around until it sees a large animal such as a honey badger. It then guides the animal to the bees' nest, stopping and calling on the way. Once the badger finds the nest and hungrily breaks it open the honeyguide can feed on the wax.

Not all woodpeckers only eat insects. Sapsuckers also drill holes in tree trunks and suck up the sweet sap (sugary liquid).

Parrots, pigeons and cuckoos

Parrots, pigeons and cuckoos are all woodland birds, but they belong to different **orders**.

Parrots have often been kept as pets, because they are good at imitating human speech. Unlike most birds, they can hold food in one foot to eat it.

Parrots and their relatives

The parrot order includes cockatoos, budgerigars, lovebirds and macaws. They are noisy, colourful tropical birds that live mainly in forests. Parrots have a curved beak strong enough to crack a brazil nut and strong feet that they use to help them feed and climb.

Parrots eat plant foods: seeds, fruits, nuts and **nectar**. They often feed in large **flocks** – budgerigars feed in flocks of up to a million! Many **species** nest in holes, either in trees or in the ground.

Over 30 parrot species are **endangered**, many of them because their forest homes have been cut down. The kakapo is a rare New Zealand parrot that was almost wiped out by cats, which were brought to New Zealand by the first European settlers.

Pigeons and doves

Pigeons are a familiar sight in most towns and cities. They are feral, which means that they were once bred by people but then escaped into the wild. Doves and wild pigeons look similar to feral pigeons. They are mainly seed-eaters.

Pigeons build twig nests and lay one or two eggs. The young are born helpless, and at first they are fed on 'pigeon milk'. This is a creamy substance, which the parents make in their crops (throat pouches).

Cuckoos

Cuckoos and their relatives are a varied group, but they all have a similar kind of foot. The group includes the noisy, colourful turacos and a few larger ground birds such as the roadrunner. Cuckoos are insect-eaters. Some species specialize in eating nasty-tasting caterpillars that other animals won't eat.

Passenger pigeons were the commonest birds ever known. Over five billion of them lived in North America. But they were good to eat, so people killed them in huge numbers. The last bird died in a zoo in 1914.

About half of all cuckoo species lay their eggs in other birds' nests. The cuckoo egg hatches quickly and the cuckoo young pushes the other baby birds out of the nest. The baby cuckoo then gets all the food that the adult birds bring to the nest.

Water-carriers

Sandgrouse are desert birds related to pigeons. They have to fly long distances each day to drink. When they are first born, sandgrouse young cannot get water for themselves. So the father bird flies to a water hole and dips his belly feathers in water. These feathers are specially designed to soak up water. He then flies back to the nest and the young suck water from the feathers.

Is it a bird?

Today there are no other animals that could be confused with birds. Like birds, insects and bats can fly. But insects have no feathers or beak and most are too small to be mistaken for birds. Bats have furry bodies and leathery wings rather than ones made from feathers.

Millions of years ago, in the Cretaceous period (between 145 and 65 million years ago), things were not so straightforward. There were some early types of bird, such as *Archaeopteryx*, which had feathers and wings. But there were also other animals that could fly and other animals that had feathers. The other flyers were winged reptiles called pterosaurs, which had wings made from leathery skin. The feathered animals were certain **species** of dinosaur, which could not fly but were covered in feathers.

Pterosaurs

Pterosaur means 'winged lizard'. Pterosaurs were the first large flying animals. They first appeared when dinosaurs still roamed the Earth. Their leathery wings were supported mostly by an enormously long fourth finger bone. The other three fingers formed a claw on the joint of the wing.

Rhamphorhynchus *was a pterosaur. It had a long, bony tail to help it steer. The elongated fourth 'finger' held the leathery wing stiff.*

There were many different pterosaurs. Some had teeth and jaws like other reptiles, but some had a toothless, beak-like jaw. The biggest pterosaurs were really huge. *Quetzalcoatlus* measured 12 metres from wingtip to wingtip: as big as a small plane! The largest pterosaurs probably spent most of their time soaring and gliding, but the small pterosaurs could flap their wings and fly quite well.

Feathered dinosaurs

In recent years, many **fossils** of dinosaurs that have feathers have been found in China. These dinosaurs could not fly. They looked similar to small relatives of *Tyrannosaurus rex*, but with a feathery covering.

The fossils are about 125 million years old, which is several million years younger than the fossils of *Archaeopteryx*. So these dinosaurs were living at the same time as the **ancestors** of today's flying birds.

An artist's idea of how Archaeopteryx *might have looked. Unlike modern birds,* Archaeopteryx *had claws on the front of its wings. These might have helped it to climb trees.*

Glossary

adaptation gradual change over many years by a living thing to fit into the place where it lives

ancestor relative from long in the past

breed when a male and female living thing mate and produce young

camouflage colouring and markings that blend in with the background

class in classification, a large grouping of living things (e.g. birds), smaller than a phylum but larger than an order

colony large group of animals or plants, often of the same species, living together in a small area

digestive system part of an animal's body (stomach, intestine, bowel) that breaks down food so that it can be absorbed into the body

endangered when an animal or plant species is in danger of becoming extinct (dying out)

family in classification, a grouping of living things (e.g. gulls and terns), larger than a genus but smaller than an order

flock large gathering of birds, usually of one species

fossils remains of ancient living creatures (usually formed from bones or shells) found in rocks

genus (plural **genera**) in classification, a grouping of living things that is larger than a species but smaller than a family

kingdom in classification, the largest grouping of living things (e.g. animals)

mate verb, to create young; noun, an animal's partner

migration when birds that live for part of the year in one place move to another part of the world for the rest of the year

nectar a sweet liquid produced by flowers

order in classification, a grouping of living things (e.g. ducks, geese and swans) that is larger than a family but smaller than a class

passerines largest order of birds (includes crows, finches, sparrows, and wrens)

phylum (plural **phyla**) in classification, a grouping of living things (e.g. chordates) that is larger than an order but smaller than a kingdom

prey animal that is hunted for food by another animal

species in classification, the smallest grouping of living things (e.g. herring gulls) that are all similar and can reproduce together

vertebrates animals with backbones

Further resources

Books

Birds of Britain and Europe, J. Gooders (Kingfisher Books, 2001)
This is a practical guide to over 400 species of bird in Britain and Europe. Information on each bird includes complete checklists of features and detailed close-ups for correct identification.

DK Explorers: Birds, Jill Bailey and David Burnie (Dorling Kindersley, 1992)
This reference book looks at different aspects of birds, such as feathers, flight and nests.

Life Processes: Classification, Holly Wallace (Heinemann Library, 2000)
A look at classification across the whole animal kingdom.

Young Naturalist Guide to Songbirds, J. P. Latimer, Karen Stray Nolting and Virginia Marie Peterson (Houghton Mifflin, 2000)
A more detailed guide to the largest group of birds, the songbirds.

Useful addresses and websites

National Audubon Society
700 Broadway, New York, NY 10003 USA
Tel: (212) 979 3000 Fax: (212) 979 3188
www.audubon.org/educate/expert

Natural History Museum
Cromwell Road, London SW7 5BD UK
Tel: 020 7942 5011
www.nhm.ac.uk

Royal Society for the Protection of Birds
The Lodge, Sandy, Bedfordshire SG19 2DL UK
Tel: 01767 680551
www.rspb.org.uk/youth

Index